Having a highly engaged workforce
is the first thing required to win on
the global stage.

~ Jim Owens, retired CEO, Caterpillar Inc.

Dedication

While businesses continue to work to improve and sustain high levels of
commitment, effort, and loyalty (today called *employee engagement),* we both
are fortunate to have had these behaviors personally modeled for us –
beginning more than fifty years ago. In gratitude of that,
we dedicate this book to our parents ...

Roger and June Gareau
and
Al and Marion Lucia

Thank you for your unconditional love and support. We have been truly blessed by
your unselfish commitment to family, continuous hard work and extra effort,
and loyalty to family values. Thanks for starting and staying engaged!

Finally, we would like to acknowledge and say a heartfelt thank you to our amazing wives –
Pat and Michele – whose quiet acts of love and selflessness made writing this book possible.
We started counting some of the ways they have helped drive *our* engagement on
this book – from brainstorming with us at the dinner table and when driving
to various places, to sacrificing family time so we could write (and rewrite),
and for sharing our excitement as we reached the completion milestone.
They far surpassed 180 ways a long time ago. Thank you both for loving us –
just the way we are!

180 Ways to
BUILD EMPLOYEE
ENGAGEMENT

How to Maximize Your Team's Commitment, Effort, and Loyalty

Brian Gareau and Al Lucia

WALKTHETALK.COM

WALKTHETALK.COM

Resources for Personal and Professional Success

To order additional copies of this handbook, or for information
about other WALK THE TALK® products and services,
contact us at
1.888.822.9255
or visit
www.walkthetalk.com

180 Ways to Build Employee Engagement

The WALK THE TALK® Company
P.O. Box 210996
Bedford, TX 76095
972.899.8300

WALK THE TALK books may be purchased for educational, business, or sales promotion use.

Printed in the United States of America
10 9 8 7 6 5 4 3

$10.95
ISBN 978-1-935537-92-2
51095>

9 781935 537922

Contents

*E*mployee engagement has been about believing that the culture of the company is as important as the product.

~ Amy Pascal, Sony Pictures

Introduction

Think back to your childhood for a moment. Mom or Dad was frustrated and frantically looking all over the house for something. Finally, he or she found "it" and lamented:

Why is it ALWAYS in the last place I look?

Employee engagement is a lot like that. Businesses continue to look for competitive advantages. They benchmark. They build new buildings and invest in new technology. They outsource and work to get "lean." They hire consultants, attend seminars, and struggle to manage rapid change.

Then some of these organizations stop, think, and begin to actively involve a natural resource that has ALWAYS been there – their employees.

They go beyond theory and concept to practical application and values-based behavior. The result: they unleash extra commitment, effort, and loyalty – the three components of engagement – from their workforce. This engagement helps accelerate productivity, innovation, customer service, quality, and many other key business metrics.

Here are just a few highlights from the volume of studies done globally which show a positive relationship or correlation between employee engagement and business performance …

- Highly engaged employees <u>outperform</u> their disengaged colleagues by 20-28%. *(The Conference Board)*

- Engaged employees generate 40%+ more <u>revenue</u> than disengaged ones. *(Hay Group)*

- 84% of highly engaged employees believe they can impact the quality of their company's work product compared with 31% of the disengaged. *(Towers Perrin)*

- 70% of engaged employees indicate they have a good understanding of how to meet customer needs, while only 17% of nonengaged employees say the same. *(Right Management)*

- 68% of the highly engaged believe they can impact costs in their job or unit versus 19% of the disengaged. *(Towers Perrin)*

- Engaged employees take an average of nearly 60% fewer sick days per year than disengaged employees. *(Gallup)*

- Engaged employees are 87% less likely to leave the organization than the disengaged. *(Corporate Leadership Council)*

Now, consider these two findings:

- Almost 80% of today's organizations' market value comes from intangible assets (brand, intellectual property, and quality of workforce). *(Brookings Institute)*

- 75% of leaders have no engagement plan or strategy – even though 90% say engagement positively impacts business success. *(Accor Services)*

So, why is it that so many leaders make employee engagement a low priority? Why don't they hold themselves and others more accountable for engagement? In many cases it's simple – they either don't *want* to or don't know *how* to. This book is designed for members of that latter group. And it's for all those leaders who get … that strategy and plans without people executing them fall short of expectations … that great products without people providing quality service will not build customer loyalty … that competitive wages and benefits are not the only things that motivate employees. This book is for them. This book is for YOU!

We've combined our collective experiences in consulting, dialoguing, researching best practices, and sharing lessons learned from truly successful organizations. And we've condensed these experiences into 180 practical ideas for growing and sustaining employee engagement.

Your reading time investment is about to be rewarded with more specific ideas, action items, and behaviors for building employee engagement than you'll find in most other books on the subject. The information is presented in eight chapters – each focusing on one of eight key strategies for maximizing your team's commitment, effort, and loyalty.

But all this proven and practical information does come with a catch. As written, the strategies presented in this work are just words ... only good ideas. **You have to put them into action in order for their value and benefits to be fully realized.**

The first step in building employee engagement is for YOU to become engaged in the process.

Do that and you will have earned the right to expect others to follow your lead.

Read on. Take action. **GET ENGAGED!**

Let Values Be Your Guide

When organizational and personal values are brought to life, employee engagement often follows. This is because following values – walking the talk – builds trust, and that trust produces leaders who are respected and followed. Then, it's a short trip to employee engagement because of the positive work environment that is created.

With few exceptions, all employees want to contribute to and be part of something special, noble, good and right. And they want to work for good people whom they respect. Being values-driven – applying the ideas and strategies that follow – will help you meet both of these employee needs.

1. **Show that you value the ideas and opinions of team members,** especially those who enhance and support organizational values.

2. **Target what's out of sync.** Identify, address, and correct specific behaviors that do not support the values of your organization. This can include behaviors that negatively affect both internal and external customers.

3. **Make sure you walk the talk.** Earn the right to hold others accountable to high standards by meeting them yourself. *Rank has its privileges* – but never when it comes to lapses in integrity or values-based behavior.

4. Be sure to **clarify your instructions and other communication** by using specific language so that everyone is on the same page. It's difficult to *walk the talk* when the "talk" is either unclear or confusing.

5. **Check first.** Make sure your decisions reflect and support organizational values *before* you implement them. If there is a conflict, pursue alternatives that are a better match with stated values.

6. **Teach them.** Be sure that all the training you provide *(or arrange for)* not only teaches the mechanics of the job, but also focuses on doing the work in value-driven ways.

7. **Add a caveat.** When planning projects and activities, write down what you intend to accomplish, then add the phrase *"... in a way that reflects and supports our organizational values."* Evaluate your final plans and eventual results against this add-on criteria.

8. **Immediately address "values violations"** – any behaviors that conflict with organizational values. Do this by both pointing out the violation and holding the individual accountable for correcting it.

9. **Keep it real.** Receiving direction from your leader with unrealistic time frames can lead to values "shortcuts." So, make sure the time frames you set for assignments and projects are "doable." Ask team members for their input ... and adjust accordingly.

10. **Be dependable and deliver on your promises.** Keep a record of your commitments. Check it periodically and make sure you follow through on your word.

11. **Discuss them.** Make sure all team members are familiar with your organization's values. Talk about them at meetings and during coaching sessions. Ask each person to describe the values ... in their own words.

12. **Behavior and values congruity rocks!** Point out to your team that connecting the two makes for a more content and fulfilling life because they are then being true to themselves.

13. **Clarify your expectations.** Make sure each of your team members knows and understands that behaving according to organizational values is an expectation in your work unit.

14. **"Catch" people practicing values.** Pay attention to examples of team member behavior that is in sync with values. Then reinforce these behaviors by providing recognition or a positive comment. If you miss noticing and reinforcing them, they may not continue.

15. **Have a "what our values mean to me" discussion** with your team. Give out small prizes for … most touching, most unexpected, most profound, etc. Be creative!

16. **Include values in your performance feedback.** Build "values-driven behavior" into all the performance discussions and evaluations you conduct with team members. Ask each person to cite ways he or she has supported key principles.

17. **Include values in your hiring criteria.** Add questions to your interviews such as, *We are big on creativity here. Can you give me an example or two of how you have demonstrated creativity in the past?*

18. **Include values in your promotion criteria.** Select team members for advanced positions based not only on *what* they have accomplished *(results)*, but also *how* they accomplish those things *(values-driven behavior)*.

19. Enlist your staff in a "Values Patrol." Solicit their commitment to tell each other (including you) whenever they observe behaviors or decisions they believe are out of sync with organizational values. Have fun with this. Appoint a "Values Officer" for important meetings. Supply him or her with a toy police badge and a whistle to blow when values violations are observed.

20. WWTMVDPIKD? When deciding how you will respond to challenging situations, answer this question:

What Would The Most Values-Driven Person I Know Do?

Picture that person in your mind. Envision him or her responding to what you are facing. Then do the same thing!

> *It's not hard to make decisions*
> *if you know what your values are.*
>
> ~ Roy E. Disney

21. Examine your policies. Ask team members to identify any policies, rules, or guidelines that make it difficult for them to do their jobs in values-driven ways. (Yes, such obstacles *do* exist – probably more than you think!). Change those that you control; try to influence a change for those that are beyond your authority.

Communicate Your Way to Commitment

Most employees want to know *where* their organization is going, *why* it wants or needs to go there, *how* they can make meaningful contributions, and *what* are the potential personal benefits to be gained by supporting the business and its goals. The more they understand those things, the greater the likelihood that they will be committed to, and engaged in, their jobs. And the way you, as a leader, help team members develop that understanding is through **communication.**

Your ability to communicate effectively is critical to your employees' success. Your messages – and the way you deliver them – can encourage team members to more readily accept feedback, share ideas for improvement, take more personal ownership of their jobs, and be more engaged in the things they do.

Here are several communication tips that should prove useful ...

22. **Expand your personal communication to 1-2-3.** 1) Share information in a timely manner through oral, written, and/or electronic means. 2) Enhance understanding of the information by describing how employees should apply it in their daily activities. 3) Reinforce key messages through repetition.

23. **Speak louder than your words.** Effective body language can increase understanding. Facial expressions, hand gestures, posture, and eye contact can give your employees a better feel for the sincerity and passion *behind* your words.

24. **Shift into positive.** An upbeat tone of voice can increase the confidence, certainty, and commitment of your employees. Pay attention to *what* you say AND *how* you say it.

25. **Address the "Triple I."** Share personal stories with your staff that exemplify **Identity**, **Importance**, and **Impact**. *Identity* addresses pride to be part of the organization/team. *Importance* emphasizes the criticality of following procedures, processes, and organizational values. *Impact* expands employees' appreciation for their roles on the team and the positive differences they can make.

26. **Create a common language.** Clearly define key terms and acronyms your team must understand in order to communicate effectively and maximize their performance. Ask and compare your staff's definitions of common business terms like: *superior customer service, quality, ROI, accountability, respect, teamwork,* and *integrity.*

27. **Be a good people reader.** Observe and "read" your employees' body language. Are they preoccupied? Do they look confused or frustrated? Or are they making eye contact with you, nodding their heads, smiling, and taking notes?

28. **Encourage note-taking.** Ask employees to write down key words, phrases, and ideas to help them remember important information. Retention is significantly higher when an individual sees, hears, *and* writes something down versus just hearing or seeing it. Note-taking also enhances focus and attention.

29. **Check for key message transfer.** Ask employees to describe (in their own words) the key "take away's" from your communication. If they did not retain the information you desired, take time to clarify and then recheck.

30. **Whattaya thinkin'?** Encourage participation by soliciting team members' opinions, feelings, and concerns. Focus on *what* is said, not *who* said it. When people get things off their chest, they tend to feel better and can then better focus on the task at hand.

31. Be "in the moment" when talking to people. Keep distractions at a minimum so you can really listen to what is being said … and how it is being conveyed.

32. Avoid multitasking during phone calls (e.g., doing e-mails while on a conference call). It's disrespectful and can send a message that something else is more important than the caller. Give your undivided attention.

33. Listen carefully to people's opinions. What people perceive influences how they act or behave. If individuals don't believe their opinions are valued, why would they offer suggestions on ways to improve the business?

34. Pause! Allow enough "think time" between asking your question and receiving a response. Sometimes we get impatient and either ask additional questions, or even worse, offer our opinion. Short-term silence is okay – even desirable. But if it continues beyond the point of comfort, try rephrasing the original question.

35. No disappearing! Allow employees to listen but not disappear from the discussions. Some people are naturally quieter than others – that's okay. But everyone has an opinion. Encourage team members to share and participate by using questions like: *Does everyone agree? … Any different perspectives? … Why might people feel that way? … Has anyone ever run into this type of situation before?*

36. Try "The X7 Strategy"! Identify your most critical messages and repeat them seven times over a one-month period – using different communication techniques and media. The more you reinforce key messages, the more your people will understand what's truly important … and remember it!

37. **Name that tune.** Tie music to goals, objectives, and initiatives as a memory anchor. Music is retained significantly longer than the spoken word. For example, if you want people to remember to create a good customer experience, you might connect the song "Good Vibrations" by the Beach Boys to your goal. The message: Let's create good vibrations for our customers.

38. **Put 'em in pictures.** Document as many initiatives, events, and milestones as possible with pictures and videos. This will help connect people emotionally. And their positive feelings will drive engaged behavior.

39. **Know when it's time to *stop* asking questions.** When people are extremely uncomfortable, they usually will show it – and often shut down. Pushing for answers and/or interrogating someone, at that moment, could create long-term disengagement and mistrust.

40. **Provide timely responses to questions and concerns.** This simple behavior demonstrates genuine interest and concern. Employees who believe their leaders care about them as individuals will give those leaders more commitment, effort, and loyalty.

41. **Don't hold questions until the end.** Build periodic Q&A breaks into your meetings. Avoid waiting until the end. Too often, time runs out and this important engagement activity gets shorted.

42. **Develop and apply e-mail standards.** Increase the use of consistent instructions in the "subject" field. Examples: "FYI," "Action Requested," or "Please See Me." Help people understand when "cc" and "bcc" should and should not be used. These simple techniques can enhance work effort – a key desired outcome of engagement.

43. **Pay attention to jokes and cartoons.** Look at what employees post in their work areas or share with coworkers. These communications may give you clues on things that are frustrating and disengaging your team.

44. **Require everyone to practice electronic device etiquette.** Cell phone, BlackBerry®, and PC use during meetings can be very distracting and disengaging. Create a work environment in which listening and dialogue are expected and highly valued.

45. **Avoid "data dumps."** Narrow communications down to no more than three key points. Bombarding team members with more information than they can handle or absorb increases the likelihood that they'll tune out.

46. **Don't shoot messengers.** Avoid coming down on team members who inform you of problems or setbacks. When it comes to leadership, ignorance is NOT bliss. You can't deal with and fix what you don't know is broken. Making employees feel bad for keeping you informed is NOT the way to enhance their engagement.

> *The most important thing in communication*
> *is to hear what ISN'T being said.*
>
> ~ Peter Drucker

Full Engagement Requires Getting 4 Things RIGHT

1. Doing the **Right THING**
   (action aligned to goals and values)

2. Doing it at the **Right TIME**
   (timeliness – when needed and appropriate)

3. Doing it the **Right WAY**
   (according to rules, procedures and policies)

4. Doing it for the **Right REASON**
   (commitment vs. compliance)

Here's a behavior analysis chart that helps answer the question, "Do we have full engagement?" Only the last example shows full engagement (indicated with a + symbol).

Example	Right THING (Y/N)	Right TIME (Y/N)	Right WAY (Y/N)	Right REASON (Y/N)	(+/-)
Gain consensus with peers (but <u>only</u> because your boss is in the room)	YES	YES	YES	NO	(-)
Attend mandatory meeting (but arrive late, and do other work during meeting)	YES	NO	NO	NO	(-)
Take extra time to listen to customer, explore options, and resolve issue	YES	YES	YES	YES	(+)

Focus on Relationships

As a leader, you have a great deal of influence on the way people do their jobs – and the level of commitment they exhibit in the process. How you *interact* with them affects how they *act* and perform, every day.

To be sure, your team members are employed by the organization – but they work for *you*. They take direction from *you*. They have relationships with *you*. And it's the quality of those relationships that ultimately determines whether they show brightly or merely show up. The more positive your relationships with the people you depend upon, the more trust and loyalty you will earn – and the more employee engagement you will experience and enjoy.

Here are some things you can do to make that happen …

47. When making decisions, **build consensus and support** by finding what's in it (the benefits to be gained) for as many team members as possible – and sharing that information with everyone. This will lead to better agreement, harmony, and more win/win situations.

48. **Develop a positive "grapevine."** Instead of letting negative rumors flourish, stop the spread of incorrect information. Share the facts and emphasize the positives. Doing so will enhance trust and good feelings within your work group.

49. **Minimize communications that begin with "why"** (e.g., *Why did you bypass that policy?).* They tend to produce defensive reactions. Instead use questions like: *Do you agree that following the policy would have helped you?* This approach fosters adult-to-adult dialogue which is critical to building and maintaining productive relationships.

50. When discussing issues, **use open-ended questions** – ones that cannot be answered with a mere yes or no. Probing with questions like: *Can you tell me about it?* or *Why do you suppose that happened?* tends to engage the person in a true conversation and enhances relationships by demonstrating that you truly are interested in what he or she is thinking.

51. **Provide periodic feedback on performance and behavior.** Let team members know how they're doing and how they measure up to your expectations. The additional "security" that comes from people knowing where they stand leads to better relationships and a trust that you will "level" with them.

52. **Provide a spark.** Encourage employees to move from passive engagement (e.g., attend a meeting) to active engagement (e.g., participate in the meeting). Let them know that their ideas are valuable and important – but can't be considered if they aren't presented.

53. **Seek out and nurture committed relationships** – a cadre of family, friends, and employees who help at those inevitable times of need. Spend time with coworkers, friends, and family members whose values connect with yours. Better relationships can lead to more engagement because of the desire to help each other.

54. **Sponsor family-inclusive events and activities.** These can be effective relationship builders. Be sure to involve team members in the planning and operation.

55. **Capture "a few of their favorite things."** Learn what team members like and really care about. Bake these into your recognition – like a handwritten note for one … or coffee with another. This can create more meaningful recognition for the receiver and enhance the relationship you have with him or her.

56. **If you adopt employees' ideas and suggestions, give them credit.** If you don't, explain why. This will keep the ideas coming and encourage individual participation and engagement.

57. **Use your ears.** Listening is one of the most powerful ways to build and strengthen relationships. It's a demonstration of respect. When you listen to others, you're nonverbally saying, *Your thoughts and ideas are important … Your concerns are important … YOU are important.*

58. **Help them develop.** Create opportunities for team members to learn, grow, and expand their skills and experience. Demonstrate that you and the organization are looking out for your employees, and they'll be more likely to reciprocate.

59. **Respect their time.** If you want employees to believe that their work is important, you have to believe it, too. More importantly, you have to behave like you believe it! Don't expect people to drop whatever they're doing every time you need something. Instead, ask if they have a few minutes to chat. Better yet, ask for a time when they'll be available to meet with you.

60. **Explain "whys" as well as "whats."** Unless there is a legitimate need for confidentiality, always tell team members the reasons behind decisions, assignments, instructions, procedures, and changes. This adult treatment enhances relationships and builds commitment for what needs to be done.

61. **Spread "the wealth."** Rotate the drudge work and less-desirable tasks so that everyone shares part of the load. Likewise, spread around the prime, high-profile assignments so that every team member has an occasional opportunity to shine brightly.

62. **Make personal sacrifices for the welfare of others.** Work/cover someone's shift … take on the "dirty job" … go out in the storm to get pizza for the crew that's working late – and watch the relationships you have with your people flourish.

63. **Admit mistakes, correct them, and move on.** No one is perfect. Employees tend to have greater respect for leaders who own up to their errors. And respect is a key building block for productive relationships.

64. **Socialize.** Eat lunch or take a break in the cafeteria and/or common area with others – not at your desk – whenever possible. This type of activity will further open lines of communication and show your human side. In general, people work better for those they know.

65. **Address and stop inappropriate sarcasm, destructive humor, and bullying.** Employees are counting on you to make sure the work environment is safe, positive, and respectful.

66. **Get some feedback.** Ask your team members two questions:
What do I do that helps you accomplish your work?
What do I do that hinders your work or makes it more difficult?
Continue doing the positive actions and attempt to eliminate as many of the "barriers" as possible.

67. Take time to have conversations and **develop a relationship with the person you report to.** Both of you can learn from each other's experiences and perspectives – and you'll likely experience greater levels of mutual appreciation.

68. **If you don't know something, admit it.** Then go and research the answer. People respect that kind of straightforward, honest approach. Honesty is another building block of positive and productive relationships.

69. **Keep them informed.** Make sure team members have the information they need and want. Take special care to do this on subjects of direct interest to them in getting their jobs done. People feel respected when they're kept "in the loop" – and that feeling will likely have a positive effect on your relationship with them.

70. **Administer procedures fairly and equitably.** If leaders are not consistent with things like overtime notices, time-off requests, and performance reviews, employees may perceive "favoritism" which erodes relationships and engagement.

The glue that holds all relationships together
is trust ... and trust is based on integrity.

~ Brian Tracy

Ouch! These Behaviors Hurt Engagement!

[X] Minimizing leader visibility and accessibility.

[X] Responding to questions with "I'll get back to you" – but never following up.

[X] Creating a "fuzzy" strategy and plan of action.

[X] Having unclear roles and responsibilities.

[X] Blaming and shaming people for mistakes.

[X] Focusing only on WIFB (What's In It For The Business).

[X] Surveying people but taking no action on the feedback.

[X] Making people feel they can be easily replaced.

[X] Creating extended periods of working/life imbalance.

[X] Talking in "code" and using acronyms that many do not understand (especially regarding financials).

[X] Brushing off business losses and mistakes.

[X] Criticizing and degrading your competitors.

[X] Conducting long "death by PowerPoint" meetings.

[X] Cutting corners and undercutting people.

[X] Micro-managing.

[X] Continuing to have employees perform menial tasks after the special cost-cutting efforts are over.

[X] Compromising standards for health and safety.

Concentrate on Change

Change is inevitable and, unfortunately, so is its potential for anger, confusion, fear and uncertainty. When you add the fact that often people are being removed from their comfort zones, you can understand how engagement might suffer. Let's face it, it's tough to be engaged with what you perceive as a "moving target" – especially one that is creating insecurity or fear.

Leaders can have a significant impact on how team members deal with change – and the spillover impact on engagement as well. You can minimize those natural obstacles to engagement by helping people understand, accept and work through change more effectively and less painfully. Here's how …

71. **Share what you know.** Send clear messages about upcoming changes. Include *when, how* and *who* is affected and in *what* way. When messages involving change are cascaded through your organization, they need to be delivered with clarity and detail.

72. **Avoid using "killer phrases"** that negatively impact success when change is happening. Examples: *That will never work … The old way was good enough … I didn't design or approve this.*

73. **Involve them in planning.** Whenever possible, involve team members in change decisions and implementation planning. Identify optional approaches and let employees select – and upgrade – the path that will be taken. Remember that people tend to support that which they help create!

74. **Embrace it yourself.** Demonstrate support for, and commitment to, any changes that are taking place. Set the tone and example for others to follow. By showing the way, you become a facilitator of change rather than a dictator, a mere messenger, or a victim.

75. Crank up *your* commitment to a higher degree – regardless of the level you are at currently. Take on an additional assignment to help a team member who is struggling with change.

76. Stay in the groove. There is a fine line between a groove and a rut. To stay on the *groove* side of things, examine the benefits of a change versus the continuation of less effective practices – and communicate those benefits to your people.

77. Separate resistance to change into two categories: Obstacles and Objections. The obstacles are things that people can't control. The objections are emotional barriers. Remove as many obstacles as possible and have one-on-one discussions about objections.

78. Address *their* issues. Meet with all individuals and groups who will be impacted by a particular change. Ask them to identify their key issues, questions and concerns. Write them down. Immediately address those issues you're prepared to discuss, and schedule a follow-up session to discuss those matters that required research and investigation on your part.

79. Enlist a "change champion." Maintain stability of your change by identifying one or more team members who can, and will, actively support the new direction – even if it was initiated at another level of the organization. Getting others on board like this ensures that the success of the change is not totally dependent on you alone.

80. What's competing? Identify competing initiatives or changes that are underway. Prioritize them, and then determine the appropriate allocation of limited resources (time, money, and people) among these changes.

81. "Connect the dots" for employees by describing how the change ties to the team's (and the organization's) mission – and how implementing the change ties to individual and team success.

82. **Examine past experiences.** Talk with employees about previous changes that went well and those that didn't. Go beyond general observations and uncover details. Learn from your past change initiatives and replicate the successful steps.

83. **Are they _really_ onboard?** Observe employee behaviors and pay attention to the _way_ assignments are carried out. Don't assume that there is commitment to change. Make sure it is real and ask about concerns. Superficial acceptance of change can indicate superficial employee engagement.

84. **Equip them to succeed.** Analyze each pending change. Create an inventory list of the training, tools and resources that team members will need to successfully implement the change and maintain the new direction. Solicit input from the team. Then start getting them what they need.

85. **Don't wait to tell them.** Negative rumors spread quickly, therefore, introduce a change as early as possible to cut off the guessing and false assumptions that inevitably develop.

86. **Be EXTRA understanding.** Remember that change is as difficult for your employees as it is for you. Most people step slowly into the unknown. There are fears to overcome, new skills to develop, new habits to acquire, and new mistakes to make and learn from. Be understanding and supportive, and your people will respond.

87. **Do some probing.** Not everyone speaks up. Actively solicit input on changes from team members. You need input to make the best decisions as a leader, and that information does not always fall in your lap.

88. **Develop a relationship with those who are initiating change** so you can get "early warnings" of what is coming and how it affects your team. Then you can plan the best strategy ... and keep your people properly informed.

89. **Speak up.** Communicate your objections and concerns to change initiators when a new direction negatively impacts team or organizational results. However, keep an open mind because there may be "bigger picture" issues that supersede your concerns.

90. **Encourage allies.** Be sure to recognize those who not only accept changes but also help bring others along.

91. **Allow some time.** Give each team member the time to emotionally accept the change even though they may have already displayed the new behaviors needed. Check back within two weeks to ensure they're still "onboard."

92. **Accentuate the positives.** Help team members see and understand the positive aspects of change activities and initiatives through group discussions. Ask the team to respond to questions such as, *What are examples of changes that have benefited us in the past?* and *If you had to identify two things that are positive about **this** change, what would they be?*

93. **Be willing to change the change.** If a new direction isn't working as you thought it would – or if a better idea surfaces in the middle of a change initiative – modify and adjust your plans accordingly.

A ship in a harbor is safe –
but that's not what ships are for.

~ John A. Shedd

Create an Empowering Environment

Empowering work environments are distinct. They clearly are "different" from their less empowering counterparts – and so are the relationships between the leaders and team members who work within them. These two groups interact differently – more productively. They share more information. They work closer together on common goals and objectives. They partner better on challenges. They exhibit a higher degree of mutual respect. And they enjoy what they do.

When leaders create this type of environment, team members feel more confident in their own judgment, abilities and potential. They feel more trusted to help solve problems, take risks, and make better decisions. They take more personal ownership and have more pride in both what they do and how they do it.

Leaders who want to drive and sustain high levels of engagement ultimately need their employees' heads (ideas), hearts (commitment), and hands (physical work). Creating an empowering work environment can help accomplish this.

Here are a few ideas to help you do that ...

94. **Set clear expectations.** Make sure all team members know that their jobs are important and come with accountabilities to achieve results. Define standards for both individual and team performance and behavior ... and clarify what they can expect from you – like tools, training, coaching, and support.

95. **Give some autonomy in how people get their jobs done.** The more control and influence employees have in accomplishing their specific job responsibilities, the more trust and confidence they feel their leader has in them.

96. **Create opportunities for variety.** Consider job rotation, special projects, customer visits, etc. Diverse work tends to be more stimulating and engaging.

97. **Keep employees informed about changes in your industry and what competitors are doing.** It's important that employees have confidence in the organization's products, services and competitive strategy. Confidence breeds hope and hope energizes engagement.

98. **Develop and use their talents.** Spend time discussing and gaining agreement on what specific skills and abilities each employee has and needs to further develop. Then allocate the appropriate time and financial resources for this development to take place.

99. **Discuss and document employees' career aspirations.** Then use this information to help set up informational interviews and job shadowing opportunities. Most employees' commitment and effort will increase if they see their leader working to help them succeed and gain greater responsibilities, rewards and recognition.

100. **Encourage pride** in belonging to your organization. Highlight the organization's history, how your products and services help people and their communities, social responsibility initiatives, awards, etc. People want to be part of a caring and winning team.

101. **Look, listen for, and reinforce positive attitudes and behaviors.** A "can-do" spirit creates better morale, and a good attitude is contagious and addictive.

102. **Draw the connections.** Describe and emphasize the linkage between what your team members do and the organization's overall goals and objectives. For example, consistently meeting daily production requirements, quality, and on-time shipments connect to an organization's goal of superior customer satisfaction.

103. **Teach and use established problem-solving techniques** to improve decision-making. For example, use *brainstorming* to generate lots of ideas, and *cause-and-effect (fishbone) diagrams* to sort ideas into categories. Many employees will be energized and give more effort if they are empowered to solve problems.

104. **Expand purchasing authority.** Give employees more decision-making authority within set parameters. This shows you trust them. Reduce approvals needed to make low-dollar purchases like basic supplies, software, or hand tools.

105. **Delegate responsibility AND authority.** If you plan on holding team members accountable for getting things done, you need to give them the authority required to make those things happen – within established guidelines and parameters. Responsibility and control go hand in hand. Separate the two and you have the basis for some serious demotivation.

106. **Debrief.** Hold "lessons learned" exchanges at key milestones of projects, initiatives, or change interventions. Ask questions like: *What would we do the same? … What would we change? … Why?* Help employees understand that mistakes will likely happen. It's learning from them and not repeating them that counts most.

107. **So what should we do?** Encourage employees to identify problems AND offer possible solutions. Engaged employees are usually more willing to play both roles – problem identifier and solver. This reinforces the potential impact they can have on the business.

108. **Make them experts.** Help every single team member become an expert at something job-related. Arrange for training, coaching, or perhaps "certification" on equipment, software, processes, etc. Then make up an **Expert Directory** that lists people and their special skills.

109. **Don't let them burn out.** Watch for and minimize long periods of extra workload. Mentally and physically exhausted employees can be less creative, effective, efficient and engaged.

110. **Completely disconnect temporarily.** Periodically, take a little personal time off – and leave your cell phone, BlackBerry®, or PC off as well. Encourage employees to do the same – using personal or vacation days. Periodically recharging your batteries is one of the best ways to stay productive and engaged.

111. **Encourage humor and laughter within your team.** Studies have shown that humor can lighten the pressures and stresses that can develop. But remember: Humor should never be malicious or at the expense of someone else.

112. **Avoid wasting time in ineffective meetings.** Make sure there is an agenda, a stated purpose of meeting, clear roles and responsibilities, deliverables, and tightly controlled time frames. Poorly managed meetings are demotivating and disengaging.

113. **Reinforce teamwork.** Clarify that every role and individual is important to the team's success. Encourage helping others, sharing information, celebrating successes, and learning from mistakes. Teamwork and empowerment go hand in hand … and they both lead to engagement.

114. **Tap into team members' ideas** for product, process, and service improvement. Research shows the more employees are engaged, the more they believe they can directly impact business results like customer service and quality.

The vision is really about empowering workers, giving them all the information about what's going on so they can do a lot more than they've done in the past.

~ Bill Gates

Recognize What You Want More Of

Unfortunately, there are more than a few "leaders" out there who have failed to understand – and therefore unleash – the power of recognition. As a result, far too many employees feel taken for granted, demotivated, and disengaged.

Recognition is a form of positive reinforcement – typically involving simple, nonfinancial gestures of appreciation like a thank you, a handshake, or a note. When leaders reinforce behaviors and results, they are more likely to be repeated. Simply stated – whatever you recognize you'll generally get more of.

Research consistently shows effective recognition drives engagement. In this world of competitive wages and benefits, recognition can be a true differentiator for organizations (and leaders) wishing to move ahead of their competition … and stay there.

Here are some ideas and strategies for making that happen …

115. **Know the difference between recognition and reward.** Many organizations have inadvertently combined these two concepts and created unintended "entitlement" programs of novelty items, gift certificates and prizes. There are limits to the financial rewards available each year – but recognition can take place without any budgetary considerations.

116. **No spectators allowed.** Communicate the expectation that giving recognition for positive contributions to organizational goals and objectives is *everyone's* responsibility. Don't let employees think recognition is the sole responsibility of leadership.

117. **Sincerity counts most.** Saying "thank you" is the simplest way to show appreciation – but it must be done *sincerely.* The perception of backhanded or insincere compliments can be very disengaging.

118. **Make it timely.** The closer your recognition is to the actual desired behavior/result, the higher the chances the behavior will be repeated.

119. **Be specific.** Provide employees with details on what specifically you appreciated and how it was achieved. Here's an example:

Great job handling that customer's complaint! You listened to her concerns, came up with a satisfactory solution, and left her feeling that she is really important to us.

120. **Match the strokes with the folks.** Some people enjoy public praise – others like private, one-on-one discussions. Some like individual recognition – others prefer team or group recognition. Ask team members about their preferences and match your delivery to the individual's preferred way whenever possible.

121. **Teach team members simple ways to recognize others.** Examples: a personal note, a posted note on the workstation, a quick phone message, a smile, and a handshake. Seemingly "small" actions can yield big results.

122. **Know what to look for.** Identify specific actions/behaviors your team must consistently do to meet its goals and objectives. These are the primary things that should be reinforced with recognition. For example, recognizing employees who help coworkers complete a task reinforces teamwork; recognizing employees who are always on time for work and meetings reinforces responsibility.

123. **Recognize employees for small, incremental improvements.** Praise should not be reserved just for big accomplishments or reaching major milestones.

124. **Post it!** Create an old-fashioned bulletin board and post information about key accomplishments. Include complimentary feedback received from customers, other locations and departments and coworkers.

125. **Don't overlook the simple and obvious.** Recognize and thank team members by taking them out to lunch. This becomes even more powerful if the employee is allowed to bring a guest.

126. **Create new recognition habits.** Put five shiny pennies in one pants/slacks pocket. Each time you sincerely thank someone during the day, move one penny to the other pocket. At the end of the day count how many pennies you moved. When you get all five moved each day for 17-21 consecutive days, you have created a habit to regularly recognize others. Encourage employees to do the same.

127. **Practice "random elements of surprise"** when recognizing individuals and teams. For example: call an impromptu stand-up meeting and celebrate a customer compliment. Most people will be energized by the break in routine.

128. **Ask their opinion** – it's a form of recognition that says, "I value your ideas and perspectives."

129. **Put them on point.** Create opportunities for team members to have direct contact and interaction with executives, customers and suppliers. Doing so reinforces that you trust your people and appreciate how they do their work.

130. **Let the "big bosses" know.** Forward complimentary e-mails about your team's performance or behavior to senior management. Add your personal congratulations and cc the team. Most people will appreciate the pride you have in them and the work they do – and your willingness to tell those who are higher up.

131. **Keep a recognition log.** For one complete week, record *who* you recognized, *how* you recognized them, and *what* specific behavior or result was reinforced. Then, analyze your list – looking for patterns and trends. Did you recognize a majority of your staff? Did you use multiple methods? Did you reinforce key organizational objectives like quality, on-time delivery, accuracy, cost control and safety?

132. **Develop tangible reminders for recognition** – like a traveling trophy, a stuffed animal, a coin and food treats (Life Savers®, Kudos® bars, etc.) These items will bring back the feeling of appreciation after the initial recognition has taken place.

133. **Celebrate important dates.** Take time to record employee birthdays and service anniversaries on your calendar. When those dates arrive, stop by and congratulate the person or send them a note, e-mail or card. And be sure to acknowledge and congratulate life events like births, graduations, weddings, children's or grandchildren's accomplishments, etc.

134. **Apply the personal touch.** Opt for handwritten notes over preprinted cards. The personal touch says you really care about the individual.

135. **Spelling counts.** Double-check the spelling of names when doing any written form of recognition (certificates, notes, etc.). This simple proofing step can be the difference between positive and negative recognition.

136. **Correct recognition mistakes.** If you inadvertently forget to include someone in your recognition, go to them, apologize, and thank them for their effort and/or accomplishment. Don't skip this important step and hope the error will simply be forgotten. Many times it will be replayed over and over, and create disengagement.

137. **Measure perceptions.** Check through surveys or simply ask employees if their work and effort are regularly acknowledged and appreciated. If the answer is no, then recognition is not yet a habit on your team. You need to ratchet up your recognition efforts.

> *Appreciate everything your associates do for the business.*
> *Nothing else can quite substitute for the few*
> *well-chosen, well-timed, sincere words of praise.*
> *They're absolutely free … and worth a fortune.*
>
> *~ Sam Walton*

I realized early on that if you create a company where employees enjoy coming to work as much as going home, and where there is a high level of engagement, mutual trust, and respect, no one can beat you.

~ Paul Silvis, co-founder, RESTEK

Help Everyone Learn and Grow

In today's rapidly-changing, technologically-advanced business world, individuals and organizations must continually learn and grow – or remain stagnant and become obsolete. Making sure the latter does not happen is one of your key leadership responsibilities. And you meet that responsibility by creating growth opportunities and by encouraging team members to continually enhance their knowledge and skills.

Obviously, helping employees learn and grow prepares them, and your organization, to meet future business challenges. But, it does more than that – it also fosters engagement. When you help people develop, it's a demonstration that you care about their success — a sign that you are engaged in their well-being. As a result, they'll be much more likely to reciprocate. What goes around *will* come around if you …

138. **Create more teachers.** Teach team members how to teach others. More teachers means that more learning and development will be available to more people.

139. **Once is not enough.** Help employees develop new skills by reinforcing the desired behavior multiple times. That's what it takes to create a new, sustainable behavior. Don't be surprised if someone doesn't "get it" right away.

140. **Teach business literacy.** One powerful way to help team members grow and be more engaged is to teach them the "business of the business." The more people understand how a successful organization is run (planning, budgeting, inventory, profit/loss, etc.), the better they'll be able to contribute.

141. **Build teams from within.** Help people pool their resources by encouraging small group planning within the team. None of us is as smart as all of us. Better results occur when we pull together.

142. **Help them learn from mistakes and successes.** When inevitable mistakes occur, work with employees to identify the key learning: "What can/will you do in the future to make sure that this error isn't repeated?" Do the same for successes. Besides congratulating employees for their achievements, ask them to pinpoint the actions and behaviors that led to their success. Encourage them to apply those same factors to future tasks and projects.

143. **Give ongoing feedback to support the learning process.** People are often not sure how they are perceived as they carry out new tasks or function in a new way.

144. **Mix it up.** When teaching or giving instructions to your team, use varied approaches like charts, stories, or Q & A. People can process information four times faster than you can speak – so you have to hold their attention.

145. **Think development.** Make training an ongoing activity. Work with each team member to craft a personal development plan. And periodically ask your people to assess their own competency levels and identify areas where they need improvement.

146. **Support leadership training.** Participate yourself, and make sure that leaders who report to you have the time to attend.

147. **Grow them with goals.** Meet with your employees every 3, 6, or 12 months to identify the results they plan to accomplish during the next time period. Set up a monitoring schedule to see how they're progressing and to help them stay on track.

148. **Divide and conquer.** Work as a team to stay abreast of technology advancements. For example, 1) Divide the reading (and reporting back) of trade and professional journals among your team; 2) Ask team members to share key learning from any workshops, webinars, or conferences they have attended.

149. **Make sure they got it.** After team members attend training, ask them to describe what they have learned. Ensure a clear understanding. They can also debrief with other team members.

150. **Create a cadre of mentors.** Identify excellent performers on your team who can share their knowledge and experience to help others learn, grow, and improve. Hook them up with people who need (or desire) skill enhancement.

151. **Get creative.** Use a variety of music, videos, games, experiential exercises, role-playing, etc. as vehicles for delivering your training messages.

152. **Explore service experiences.** Ask team members to describe positive and negative customer experiences they have had. Next, explore what turned them on or off about those experiences. Finally, encourage them to apply that learning to the interactions they have with their customers – both internal and external.

153. **Teach them to show what they know.** Regardless of how or what team members learn, the key is application. Be sure to provide and emphasize practical implementation ideas in each phase of the learning.

154. **Embrace learning yourself.** Demonstrate that you value learning in all its forms: on-the-job training, structured classes, self-study, mentoring, etc. The best way to encourage others to be continual learners is to be one yourself.

155. **Take "field trips."** Arrange for team members to visit and tour other areas within your organization. This will enhance their organizational knowledge and help them see and appreciate the "big picture."

156. **Teach them what others do.** Familiarize team members with technology and key processes used in other departments. This will better prepare them for interdepartmental activities and potential future assignments.

157. **Know what's available.** Stay informed about, and familiar with, all of the developmental resources available within your organization. This includes training classes, books, movies, certification programs, and tuition assistance. Know what's available – and know how your team members can access them.

158. **Surf the Net.** There are literally thousands of free developmental resources available on-line. Work with your fellow leaders to research newsletters, blogs, etc., that relate to what your people do. Encourage team members to subscribe to, read, and apply these no-cost developmental tools.

159. **Don't forget your value.** Teach someone what you do. Even if you don't have a mentor title, you can enjoy the same personal satisfaction.

An organization's ability to learn,
and translate that learning into action rapidly,
is the ultimate competitive advantage.

~ Jack Welch

Keep Your Finger on the Engagement Pulse

Assuming you started at the beginning of this book, you've now learned over 150 ways to build and sustain employee engagement. And hopefully, you're motivated to jump in and immediately start implementing many of the ideas you have read. However, we would not suggest this just yet. Instead, we recommend you first determine what your team's level of engagement actually is – right now.

Does your perception of, and intuition about, your team's engagement match reality? Maybe ... maybe not! *Are you overlooking any existing engagement strengths and weaknesses?* Perhaps ... perhaps not! *Could you make even better engagement decisions if you continually kept your finger on your team's engagement pulse?* ABSOLUTELY YES! So pay special attention to what comes next.

This final chapter is divided into two parts. First, you'll find common, everyday things leaders should look and listen for that indicate engagement – or disengagement – may be happening. This will help you know where you stand ... what you'll want to address and build upon. Second, we'll explore ideas and strategies for increasing the effectiveness of any structured engagement-measuring surveys your organization may be using – including how to take ACTION on the feedback you receive.

Is your team resting or exercising its commitment, effort, and loyalty? How do you know? What can you do to continually measure your employees' engagement heartbeat?

You'll find answers to those questions – and more – on the pages that follow ...

160. **Pay attention.** Are team members consistently arriving right at shift start and leaving as soon as the clock strikes quitting time? Are they applying for new jobs outside of your team? Do they physically attend meetings but mentally disconnect by not paying attention or participating? Behaviors like these are typical signs of some level of disengagement.

161. **Listen to what people are saying.** Do you periodically hear comments like: *That's a great idea. Bring it up at the meeting. They'll listen to you ... Last night, I was thinking about how we can do this even better ... Let's stay over a little bit tonight and wrap it up.* These are the types of comments engaged employees make.

162. **Feel the emotions.** Can you sense a positive energy or "buzz" on your team? Do you see team members actively helping each other? Are there significantly more smiles than stares or long faces? Are there minimal complaints and a clear focus on *what's* right versus *who's* right? Are team members laughing and celebrating business success?

163. **Check the numbers.** Look at absenteeism, attrition, and the quantity and quality of people posting for jobs on your team. If attendance is high, turnover low, and the applicant pool strong, you likely have a highly desirable, engaging work environment.

164. **Watch what they wear and carry.** Do employees willingly wear or carry items (caps, shirts, briefcases, backpacks, folders, pens, etc.) with your business name or logo on it? People who have pride in being associated with an organization tend to be more engaged in their jobs.

165. **Fill in the blanks.** Ask employees to anonymously complete the following statements:

> *Accepting employment with this organization was a _____ decision, because _____ .*
>
> *I would describe the match between my personal values and the organization's values as _____ .*
>
> *When I speak to my friends about this organization, I say it is_____ .*

Do team member responses indicate commitment and loyalty?

166. **Check for job-skills fit.** Compare team members' current job duties and responsibilities against their skills, abilities and experiences. Pay special attention to team members who may appear over-qualified for their jobs. If individuals perceive they are underutilized, their engagement could be low.

167. **Check for referrals.** Pay attention to how many team members refer potential candidates for open positions within your team. Chances are good that most of your employees know people who are looking for work or better jobs. Whether or not they refer them to your organization is an indication of their commitment and loyalty – two key elements of engagement.

168. **Do they volunteer?** Check your team's overall participation levels in recent optional or voluntary events and activities such as "lunch and learns," after-work informational meetings, social events, etc. Typically, the higher the rates of participation, the higher the levels of employee commitment and engagement.

169. **Get an "outsider's" viewpoint.** Ask a trusted peer or colleague to spend a couple of hours interacting with your team and then provide you with feedback on what he or she observed and felt. Sometimes an outsider can see more clearly what's happening than you can.

If you or your organization utilizes some type of structured employee survey to periodically measure engagement, here are some ideas to consider and implement …

170. **Provide timely feedback.** Acknowledge that you heard what employees said and confirm that their input was unfiltered and unedited. Research indicates providing timely survey feedback can have a positive impact on future engagement.

171. **Take some "soak time" with survey results.** Answer the following questions: *What was reinforced (confirmation of things you already suspected were issues)? What was a surprise? What came out stronger or weaker than you expected?* Ask your employees these same questions and compare your conclusions with theirs.

172. **Start with what's working.** Too often leaders immediately focus on the lowest scores or biggest declines. However, highest scores or biggest improvements can help you understand what strategies worked and where change was handled well. Replicate how these positive results were achieved in the areas that now need improvement.

173. **Explore the "whys" behind the numbers.** Most surveys provide you a numeric score for each question – like percentage of agree or disagree. Without follow-up dialogue with employees, you may not have a complete understanding of the reasons or drivers of the "score."

174. **Brainstorm improvement ideas.** Ask employees for potential solutions to the problems or concerns they have identified. Avoid critiquing and instead allow ideas to develop by piggybacking off one another.

175. **Go after what's doable.** Focus your efforts on what you *can* fix and change. Analyze employee feedback and identify those problem areas you actually control. Those are your primary targets for action.

176. **Develop a realistic action plan.** Avoid "biting off more than you can chew" – and remember that effective change usually comes incrementally. Plan to execute no more than two to three improvement initiatives in a 90 to 120-day time period. Doing so will make it easier to monitor and control the process – and make any midcourse corrections that may be required. You'll be more likely to have a more successful intervention, and team members will see tangible steps being taken on their concerns.

177. **Before finalizing your action plan, share it with employees.** Solicit their input and comments. Seek confirmation that your proposed actions are important and will have a positive impact on the team. And be willing to modify your plan based on the feedback you receive.

178. **Give team members progress updates** at least every 30 days. Be specific when describing what the team said and what has been done in response.

179. **Execute smooth handoffs** of action plans whenever you change jobs and/or teams. The leader replacing you needs to know what commitments have been made to the team and the status of completion. And you need to garner that same information from the leader you are replacing. Each team's engagement will be enhanced by a smooth transition of plans and implementation.

180. Share the initial survey data and resulting action plans with new employees joining your team. This will help to reinforce the importance you place on candid employee feedback – and taking thought-through actions to improve.

Not everything that can be counted counts and not everything that counts can be counted.

~ Albert Einstein

You Just Might Have Engagement If Your Employees...

✓ Offer each other help without being asked.

✓ Ask questions to be sure they understand your assignments and instructions.

✓ Correct each other in constructive ways and don't always expect issues to be handled by their leaders.

✓ Look for the positive side of changes to policies or procedures.

✓ Demonstrate a "can do" attitude instead of complacency.

✓ Participate at meetings rather than merely attend them.

✓ Follow your lead and become positive, involved role models themselves.

✓ Volunteer for special assignments and task forces.

✓ Give each other recognition for jobs well done.

✓ Seek out developmental opportunities, and present their case for budgetary expenditures in a manner that helps the organization understand the value to be gained.

✓ Pay attention to metrics and recommend ways to measure and improve results.

✓ Recommend your organization to others who are seeking employment.

✓ Demonstrate by their actions that they are proud to be an important part of what you do.

We all have ability.
The difference is how
we use it.

~ Stevie Wonder

The Authors

Brian
GAREAU

Brian is the manager of Organization Effectiveness (OE) for a Fortune 50 corporation. He has helped lead the organization's design, implementation, and measurement of employee engagement. Results include eight consecutive years of improvement – moving from 1 out of 2 employees engaged to more than 4 out of 5. Brian has also provided OE consulting services to over 150 locations, worldwide, on business culture, values, measurement, and managing change.

Al
LUCIA
CSP

Al is a nationally known and respected author, consultant, and speaker. He has written numerous books and articles on employee engagement, and has consulted with many organizations regarding this important subject.

With over 40 years of Human Resources experience, Al is considered a "lifeline" to business executives throughout the United States. He has sponsored and hosted a popular Executive Networking and Best Practices Forum for the past 14 years.

Contact Al at: *www.adlassociates.com*

About the Publisher

The Walk the Talk Company

Since 1977, our goal at Walk the Talk has been both simple and straightforward: to provide you and your organization with high-impact resources for your personal and professional success.

We believe in developing capable leaders, building strong communities, and helping people stay inspired and motivated to reach new levels of skills and confidence. When you purchase from us and share our resources, you not only support small business, you help us on our mission to make the world a more positive place.

Each member of the WalkTheTalk.com team appreciates the confidence you have placed in us, and we look forward to serving you and your organization in the future.

To learn more about us, visit **WalkTheTalk.com.**

180 Ways to Build
Employee Engagement

Other Recommended Resources

180 Ways To Walk The Customer Service Talk – 180 proven techniques to attract and retain dedicated customers. **$10.95**

180 Ways to Walk The Leadership Talk – 180 techniques to help you move from being a "boss" to becoming a successful leader. **$10.95**

180 Ways to Walk the Recognition Talk – "How to" techniques to produce positive and productive performance. **$10.95**

180 Ways to Walk The Motivation Talk - 180 practical and tactical tips to get everyone energized and motivated. **$10.95**

To learn more or to place an order,
visit www.WalkTheTalk.com

Visit WalkTheTalk.com
to learn more about our:

Leadership & Talent Development Resources

Motivational & Inspirational Books

Product Sales & Special Offers

Free Online Newsletters

✦ The Leadership Solution
✦ The Power of Motivation
✦ NEW VIP Program